MW01602526

Scanning For Tigers

Scanning For Tigers

Poems by Margot Farrington

FreeScholarPress™

ISBN: 1492918628
ISBN-13: 978-1492918622

Cover illustration, *Tiger and Astrolabe*© 2009, collage by Margot Farrington

For my sister Zoë and my brother King

Acknowledgements

I would like to thank the editors who originally published these poems in magazines, journals, and anthologies. My grateful thanks also to the Norton Island/Eastern Frontier Educational Foundation and the I-Park Foundation for providing me with time and support during work on this book.

Appearances: "Suggested By The Subway"

Arabesques Review: (Algeria) "Cloud Company," "From 'The Dream Manual,'" "Greenpoint Woman On Zebra" (originally published as "Greenpoint Woman In Print")

BigCityLit: "The Muskrat"

Broome Review: "Spring Snow"

CQ: California Quarterly "Handfuls Of Leaves"

Cadence Of Hooves: A Celebration Of Horses: "Fragment"

Canary: "If A Blackbird," "Promethea Moth"

Cimarron Review: "Woman On The Shoulder"

Crab Creek Review: "Pillow"

Innisfree Poetry Journal: "Scanning For Tigers"

Meadowland Review: "Icarus In Reverse"

Out Of The Catskills And Just Beyond: "Magicians, Kindly Honor," "The Gigantic Of Miniatures"

PoetryWales: "At Bedford And Grand," "A Walk After Illness," "Castor And Pollux At The Hack Stable," "Incident" "The Blue Tiger Reigns In The East," "Umbrella"

San Pedro River Review: "Last Leaves, Late November," "White Doe" ("White Doe" also appeared in *Canary*)

Schuylkill Valley Journal: "An Evening For Joseph Cornell"

Tiferet: "Azure," "Wild Ducks"

Large gratitude also to Galen Joseph-Hunter at WGXC 90.7 FM, and to David Weinstein and Beatrice Johnson at Art On Air International Radio for interviews and readings that include some of these poems.

Table Of Contents

I The Blue Tiger Reigns in the East

II Azure

III Spring Snow

I

The Blue Tiger Reigns in the East

Scanning For Tigers

The problem, the optometrist said,
lies with print. Eyes were never meant to read
but to scan for tigers. To scan for tigers at a

distance, shift to a close-up of one arm,
where a fallen insect uncurls, walks
among hairs. Back again to distance, alert

for stripes among the foliage. Mindful
of shadow among the shadows,
conspiracies of light. The eyes,

he said, were meant for roaming. The eyes
were meant for wildness. Print, in its ant parade,
tyrannizes. You can never look at a book

the way you look at a woman. The woman
and the tiger share a sinuous flow that lets
the eyes slip by, even as they behold.

No grasping, ever, with the woman or
the tiger, though each may imprint upon the
retina a memory that devours.

At this juncture of history, he said, rare
to see the tiger anywhere. But women!
well, ambush awaits in many a place.

So which is most dangerous? Books also
excite and inflame. Banned and burned and,
come to think of it, some women burned too.

Blake's tyger ignited him. Every hunter burns.
So we're on fire, he said lastly, from all we see.
Books and men and women turn to ashes

in the end. But the tiger remains an ember.

Suggested By The Subway

(L Train approaching Bedford Avenue in percussive mode)

Here come the impalas
leaping madly before the lion
electric and fluid as fright can make them
straining to keep to the air

the doomed women   who dance
the dance they know
cannot save them   beads at their throats
breasts shaking   their feet
eloquent in the dust

and after them   the lovers
hands locked with those they
chose   before this wave
swept them
                    and

after them tumblers and fire-eaters
dressed in torn silks
the dwarves bearing torches
everyone running   running

and O   the sound of bamboo
bent without mercy before the wind
weird   chiming clatter
that fetters   then frees the mind.

The Blue Tiger Reigns In The East

(A Brooklyn morning, Williamsburg)

You will not see him, blind to the secret
striations in the sky where he pads
undetected by you and all your kind.

Yet raise the shade whose bamboo slats
first suggest you're elsewhere, waking to the
street you thought you knew.

Pythons, those sycamores. Wayside shrine each
silvered chimney, aluminum-slathered by a
lavish hand.   Hat of water tower

shades the laborer beneath, legs akimbo in the
black paddy of the roof. Rice that fell while you
still slept, lies pearly within pigeons:

one will fly embraced
when the masterless hawk
                              stoops.
Bread, too, was tossed, brown/white/black-brown
beside a wall of cinnabar: sun-blazoned vinyl siding.

Soon
doors' collective yawn, spice of the daily
sold and strewn.   Soon
sultans. Orders. Servants hurrying and shirking.

Bamboo Grove, Huntington Garden, CA

The swathe they've incised runs four feet deep.
When wind blows, crowds of initials
click and court in the grove. Place of garden lovers,
also the turf of Wanda & Richie,
Jack 'n' Stacy forever, spot where John loves Tom.
No one's taught them bamboo's 1,400 uses,
nor that some species take 30 years to bloom,
some 100. Asian myth reveals that man
sprang from the hollow internode, but the story hasn't
reached them; they're an army of jackknives.

The satin-skinned. The restless. Would they not be
better off schooled about all the dreadful uses
someone waits to put them to? No one's here,
though I envision them, indolently carving.
Someone, risking scorn and shrugs, might
tell them what Issa said: "Rare luck it is indeed,
to be born in human form."

I am a stranger passing through,
arrested by their work. The bamboo
ripples, parts its scars to bare the place
where none have touched.
Wind again. Who bows first, myself or the bamboo?
Who at this moment can divide one
survivor from the others?

Incident

No one commented on the pomegranate
Crushed in the subway aisle, packed rubies
Scattered: whose unhinged plea was that?

No one ventured to translate strokes
Scrawled in juice: stricken message of a
Culture we'd been schooled to ignore.

We turned from its wild script to papers,
Furtive study of faces or shoes
And when that writing crawled towards us,

(Wine of slaughter in a grey rill)
For the train transmitted it—I'm lying—
It wrote by its own surge of will,

I say when that writing crawled towards us,
    We looked away.

None dipped a finger in, to mark their own
Forehead. No one paled, pointed to reveal
Someone among us. Not one of us broke

Into song foreign to our own tongue, or
Shrieked with an anguish that would have
Brought the train to trembling halt.

Midnight. We wept, comfortless. Who'd
cried aloud our name? They'd awakened us,
recalled us to some fierce and recent shame.

Ming

I

Where does he get you? Never mind, he gets you.
Just a cub as yet, but you're a fantasy fulfilled,
else why would your place be at 141st
& Adam Clayton Powell Jr. Boulevard?

There's his trip—then there's yours. You've traveled far,
tiger, past any leap your legs could take you.
Who does he think he is? Never mind, he thinks it.
And if he never dissed Kipling or read Blake,
    what of it, friend?
A childless man, he dubs you Ming, and hopes that
bell-struck sound will banish Lonely & Ordinary,
                        those sorry-ass demons.

Little Ming, mother-robbed and smuggled.
Brought to custody eight floors up.
Invent her: realtor who says, "Spacious two bedroom.
Master bedroom plus spare for you know who."

The alligator? In the bathroom, and while he fits—
in the tub. What does he feed Ming and Al?
Never mind, he feeds them. Ming burnishes in
skin and eye. The 'gator gains both weight and plate.

Your man never weighs love against obsession,
but deems you rare and choice. And what does
Man want but what no one else has? You're his
topaz, cut and polished by secrecy. Four hundred
pounds of potential: the cat out of the bag.

What does one cat say to another? He tells you all:
Ming, I this, I that...confessions sweet and beastly,
Ming languorous or restive, hearing everything.

II

Keeper of changeless measurement: walls, window, and door.
Receiver of a thousand lashes as sun and streetlight
pierce blinds. Pliant—Ming's pacing—though spirit petrifies.
And yes, there is yes, repetition elsewhere. From 8A,
same quarrel, aftermath of sobs. Driving
beat in 8C, where walls jive and floors jump. Laughter and
conversation, homey smells of cooking.

One room from Ming's, sits girlfriend's child and a
babysitter. Girlfriend's gone with Ming's captor
to eat Chinese, then party hard.

III

Cat piss? 8-B got twenty cats?
7-B grows rank. Lord, even twenty couldn't
make that smell, that sound.
Whispers. Little gatherings. Someone makes a phone call.

IV

For court, a suit and a state assemblyman
plus entourage: bodyguards—one in leather, sporting
zebra hat band. But the court's got hospital report of
bites on arm and leg, paperwork found for purchase
of leopard and bear. His lawyer messes up, misses a date.

Let fall the gavel, pronouncements:
"Reckless endangerment of a child."
"Neither remorse nor understanding."
Like doubles by dice roll, the man's ensuing
sentence: five months jail, five years probation.
Later, alligator. Al gets shipped to Indiana.
Ming's splendor ripples off to Ohio.

V

Would you hear the Song Of Ming?
Let the musicians take the stand. O
endangerment (trumpet!). O recklessness (drum!).
Zoo - whoo - whoo, the wind blows down
Harlem streets. The poor are moving out, the rich in.
Uptown's hot, and in Ohio, the tiger's digs are bigger,
but a box is a box (beat on it) a yard (say bass and piano)
keeps you to it, strict walkin' no matter how you
strut it. Ming of Worlds Awry fix us with
your implacable gaze. Roar or be mute,
'tis all one, as the playwright used to say.
Had we a world made by tigers, what might we
find? One man and woman only, in a circle
scratched in earth. One pair confined for their
species' sins in that other sphere, and the
hunger infinite upon them, the yen for space keen
upon that man (blow trumpet!) and his mate (drum!).

Boneset To My Intellect

"Boneset to my intellect" is a phrase drawn from Thoreau's writings

Hey there, Thoreau. I dig your phrasing.
   Let's take your meaning for a
swing. I'm thinking trumpet, bass,
piano, and drums. You're thinking
woods, a moccasin walk
within and without willows. You
set the pace, we'll
   trail, hurry slightly
if you signal.

Boneset. Band looked it up: said
plant with opposite leaves.
(We too oppose when the melody asks, and
grow on alternate takes).
Aster family (we read on) of
white-rayed heads, tonic powers.
Same with us,
                    up there on the bandstand.

Know you seek the Grand, the
Serene (I've dipped those streams), the
Invisible (that's the dead, making sure
   you hit your notes). And the Companion
Who Encourages (I'm picking up my horn).
Know we court solitude in spotlight,
   keep berry-ramble in this flask.
Pond and moon and immortality? Disc.   Disc.   Disc.

Woman On The Shoulder

How many times has she turned, geared for
engine sound? Our car bears down; the very

air about her seethes. Flush with boredom and
refusal, she offers herself in iron heat

while distance still deceives. Goddamn.
Goddamn. We two are women, not men.

Centuries reside in those Maybellined eyes. I swear
she turns to basalt as we pass, and walks

the road igneous. But not before I glimpse the
twister in her gaze, watch as flood tops levee after

levee. Nothing can stop her, halt the way she
recedes in the rear view mirror. But no, she

draws close. Even closer. Palmettos glint by the
gutted hotel, a lone azalea mocks. For miles

glass grinds its teeth on the verge where legions
hurl their bottles, scheming and thirsting

for what they cannot have. I wonder how this
afternoon will end, how long we stayed in sight, if I can

lie and say we were not her last chance. Not that we
could truly offer. Not that she would actually accept.

Yet I can hear the car door open despite the separating
miles, I can smell our fear and her ferocity

mingle us into one.

Dusting With The Cat

Her sinewy self, her mood, allows us our
game. I hold her loosely round the ribs
just back of the forelegs. We trace
figure eights and each
begets another. Her purring revs,
spun by turns into a vocal gleam.

She doesn't care that she's a rag, that
dust has her. We're locked in the luster of
movement, building layers like a pearl.
We're drunk on the wine of motion a
certain speed achieves. What speed I
cannot say, though the fluent cat does—
her song spliced with pauses
where the orbits intersect.

We're burnishing our years into the
surface of my desk: her proverbial nine,
my uncertain number.
But a swinging cat cares not for count,
living for sensation, and a
wild woman always believes
she has more time.

Odalisque

My hands would tremble, stealthy
as the count increased. How the
pages betrayed my silence
with their whispering!

Slowing my pace by increments
through the rising 50's, I cut their
sibilance down and down to

slink into the 60's
soundless. Heat spreading from my palms
flushed all my fingers tropic.
Damp, my grip enhanced,
I strove for nothingness

in turning. To breathe no telling
breath, to keep my chair from creaking. My
stifled heart grown huge,
heaving in its snare. Page 70, 71,
seizures of longing. Suffused at 72
by something I couldn't name, I'd

turn to page 73—both of us
startled at the same time. She from her
place upon plump cushions,
I from my world of a separate century.

Birds Witness The Fourth Of July

Roc: in Persian legend, a huge and fabulous bird of prey

Clouds from one-place thunder
drift pungently from the river.
The whistles of this hour compress us

all to one bird: we startle from branch to
branch, settle together. Behold the pinions of
mighty wings and mile-high crests. See

how suddenly sky confronts us!
Ancient, our race, we emigrated long ago,
but recall the legends of the roc. What can

this be but the roc's egg falling from ledge
to celestial ledge? The one within will
soon hatch; this Night of Nights cannot

die quiet, insistent as the hour when our
little ones fledge, as when mulberries
ripen—black ones and white ones.

See how the trees bow amid flashes,
reverent in the cooling heat.
Even the people have come to watch.

Hidalgo Drive, Los Angeles

Up rough untended hillside dips the
down-sweep of branches
weighty with pomegranates:
Babylon behind iron palings
   crying *world, world, world,*
                      and of each swung globe

ants are hopeful, and of those split, delirious.
Breeze caresses expertly, a stem says *ah!*
Feel how fruit falls for earth's
hard kiss. In the subtle aftershock, listen:
you might hear your own existence
swell. Sound of

sun struck into night and moon
grafted onto day. Of blood's coursing, of
desire set like a gem in flesh.

No wealth like pomegranates where no one
walks because everyone drives.
Pomegranates. Ablaze inside the
seraglio. If you would plunder them,
wait on twilight, come muscled and light and lithe.

Pillow

Perhaps a dream of flying
burst the seam and let them out—

this huff of down, each feather sporting
bold or subtle motley: the snow-spun,

the herringbone, the buff-and-cinnamon mix. The one
edged and eyed with indigo-licked black.

All those tiny flexible quills,
poised and rustling within. What might they

write if dipped in dream's ink and
put to flight on paper?

They might be eloquent on the foxy nature of fatigue:
how midway into sleep's slow, relaxed thaw

the body may suddenly reconnoiter.
Blurred, stealthy as spring snow, it imprints the

body beside it, each kiss losing to the next, hands
enacting one hundred hands.

First of the family of pillows were the ancient stones.
The most forgiving pillows? Belly and breast.

The least comfortable? Starved arms, folded on
hard floor. The best pillow for grief is sleep, the

most beautiful pillow, moss, growing in mounds
wherever birdsong braids with silence.

Man or woman, passions spent, rests head and listens:
hears captive feathers settle and whisper.

Remember, they say, remember your childhood cup
of green and white. The hands of your second lover,

those generous thumbs. Recall a friend betrayed,
and the day your dog was killed in the road—

how you knelt in blood, saw the driver drive on.
Remember canoeing a creek whose clarity

matched tears, where darning needles skimmed,
stitched moments to mind. Bits of past

intruding on present, whose narrow window burns
blue. Keep looking. Watch the mullioned panes

deepen, darken. Stumble, but softly. Forget.
Forget everything. Slip in the darkest fold. Sleep.

II

Azure

Icarus In Reverse

See me sucked from sea's brine, cry
returned to my mouth pulls in preceding
shriek that inhales gasp before
then there's no more nor do my wings
betray but pluck treacherous pinions—here, there,
snatched with a marvelous fury from air
feathers fly dart-wise into wax, bigger quills
double-secured by thread considered in
construction and swift as water winks at sun
wax cools to capture shafts as
threads manic and precise continue
counter-lash and knot. Don't stop—let me rise
tumbling upward to grace, gaining back
errant feathers that home like arrows to
target—their bronze boy regaining control—There!
There's the wing beat where first I faltered.
Now I soar swoopily backward, mouth open
in glee, dropping altitude till I beat by my
father's side, passing on our left
Samos and Delos, while on our right Lebynthos whizzes
by as below ploughman and shepherd share brief
cameos, one pointing, the other leaning on his
staff lest he fall down as we flap
snap/snap to the island. See us touch earth, toe to heel, my
father unkiss me, untake my face in his hands,
tears race up his cheeks.
He says: "…safe be will you and near me Keep
.them melt will heat the high too if…" and so on,
all that he says lost to the speed-slur of the tape
that pauses only if you do. Don't pause—let our
efforts be shorn from the footage, clipped
till we stand yearning at cliff's edge. You'll
sense how time clambers with us in our descent,

handhold by foothold, our labors
collapsing inward, crazed and intent.
I beg you, hurry. Again, Minos imprisons us.
Faster! Let the thing be done. I prefer
this grounding to the flying. Prefer my
father's anguish to my own dying.

Castor And Pollux At The Hack Stable

Castor and Pollux (Gemini, the twins): Castor was famous for training and managing horses.

Centuries later, we stroll the aisle of this stable,
you and I invisible, peering into the stalls

out of our time, beyond our depth to be able
to do much beyond looking. And it galls

me beyond words to confront these unfortunate
mounts fated to endure whoever pays

to ride them. Look at this dull-coated mare, scorched
of her spark, the scarred knees on that bay—

who did that? He's gaunt, too, as is this pony
lifting his head to lip my hand. Their stingy

master shorts them, I would say, on oats. Hay only.
Smell it? Moldy. Outside the wind's astringent,

sleet horizontal. Mud in the stableyard lies fetlock deep.
A misery that foals mercy: no one will ride today.

Pollux, did you ever guess we'd leap
Beyond the hard-fought fields? In the fray,

superbly mounted, we'd help one side or the other.
(We switched often, as I recall). Lake Regillus,

remember that? Our fame growing, Grecian brothers
by then gone Roman. "White as snow their armor was,

their steeds were white as snow." Macaulay. Welding
our glory into verse. Lines carved into a plinth,

actions having ended prior. Watch out—that gelding's
got his ears laid flat. Give him room; he's sickly with

rage; I know the signs. I know he's suffered hugely here
Mixed with the good warm odor of horses, I smell

something else: the frosted metallics of fear.
As if I heard, struck from celestial anvil, a knell

for where the future lies, hammered out of true. Its curve
straightened, the holes to keep it fastened filled.

I don't just mean for these horses, striving to swerve
the worst. Nor us, put out to pasture in star-spill.

I mean this planet, by whose heavens we keep our place.
The farther it distances me, dear brother, the more

I've come to love Earth. The less use the human race
maintains for our story, the more I want to implore

them to keep us. What should we be—and they?—if torn
from that connection? Where should we ride in the blue

vaults of space if struck from memory? We're forlorn
enough in the face of changes, our public aloof,

less literate now: palm-piloted, flat-screened, ear-phoned.
To many, a lyre is one who lies. They are not taught

as we were. Their lives are not Euclidean, not honed
into a shape to serve them well. They face an onslaught

we stare upon, incredulous. Look, Pollux! Every horse
has put head over stall door to listen to me worry.

Look at their eyes, clairvoyant in the force
of how they regard us: Leda's twins, the Dioscuri,

as sad as they. As weary. Welcoming of the precious nights.
I can almost hear each heart, stoic in each great chest.

Azure

The sky hides a puzzle. You must be a
missing bit. Dropped by heaven-hand to
beguile and lead me astray.
Where are we going? White violet, you say.
Why haven't I lived my life
riveted to your flutter? You beat as if you
knew my heart by heart. Memorized every
second that ever gave me joy.
Where are we going?
Old field cinquefoil, you answer.
Yellow, yellow, yellow, calls a bird
intimate with the plan. You rise, dip towards
shoreline where sea enfolds sky.
The jut of coast cuffed with stone and
sleeved by wild flag in bloom.
Was there a thing called winter?
Sorrow-kite, break string and fly.
I am an iris among irises
lofting into butterfly, and we are
firmly under sail and I have left two feet
ashore. Farewell, faithful servants who
carried me thus far.

An Evening For Joseph Cornell

This blue? Your trademark shade, deepening tint by
tint. Sparing with your stars, only three may be
viewed at the moment: two in close communication,

a third, lonely and far. You are that third star, gazing
upon chosen trees: sinuous beech, rough oak
an owl grasps. All of your owls like candles set
in the sconces of forests, their gaze a
mirror of your own, insomniac of longing.

Coolness releases the fragrance of clover,
white campion, and grass. Slowly it moves through
twilight as your hand once did, the time you
slid a bouquet to the pretty girl
in the movie box office. Your somber face and

blooming hand her best surrealist dream.
Unsure she was awake, she screamed—
such homage too unsettling.

Tonight she discovers herself in a box made for one of
your starlets: nymph by the edge of the pool, poised to
flee. Moonlight makes her the
birch apart from the circle
straight and slant, conspiring to stand as
white Roman numerals.
The hour cupped in chimes unheard. The lover waiting.

The Premonition

Whose flat rooftop
was this?
What made it rise?
Within chalked squares I stood
giddy, and let their
geometry slide. My gaze left my shoes, lifted into
summer sky.

              Not a cloud. Not a bird.
Abruptly, confusing leaves intruded in
marvelous detail: I noticed that these were made of
amber or carnelian, lit by
sun in such a way, they hooked my breath—
pierced,
set,
and reeled my heart away.

Surely this was autumn,
autumn as never before. Too late for forgiveness,
and tinged with terror. The scene
shifted;
I ran forward to leap some gate
I wouldn't make.

I didn't jump it—I
dodged instead, conscious of narrowing space.
Cried out. Woke to the
steeplechase of tears down my face.
Who loved or didn't love me? Darkness wouldn't say.

To Anesthesia

Often I heard your name, wondered if we
might meet, heiress of millions.

So this is your room—tell me before I forget
which angel advised on the lighting, and who
designed the table. Lots of servants here. *Not too far
up*, someone says. *Your head goes there.* I find the
hollow, stretch out my arms. Yes, tie me, please,
since I'm unclear on our departure, and about how
long we'll be away.

Oh, Anesthesia, such a stare and from such distance.
Give me your hand—sorry, I meant take mine. And say
something, if not in your own voice then in the voice of
someone present. *What is it you do?* someone
asks, he who ties one wrist. Should I tell him? How
insufficient it sounds; it must be a lie, my life. Listen

not to what I say, but divine what dogged me to
this place, what cannot be cut away. We're
detained by these others, your orders silent, efficient, your
strategy laid with this heated blanket, warmed as you
await me, as your servants smile, and the gleam of silver
waits under white folds.

But Anesthesia, why tell you, who has had so many,
loved some for keeps?
The two who know your wishes best
approach, and one smiles. At once I know I have
permission to speak to you, and I summon the

breath to say it, and suddenly we're alone, so private
in your spell, I'm milkweed on the wind,
floating upon your listening to the
sound of my heart. Your head is pressed against
my breast; I am about to say I love you, we stand
in a black spotlight illuminating the hour.

We must be going, you say, *we must be
going* ... already the spun miles court silence.
How slow I am, who nonetheless keeps pace—
one hand in yours, the other closed around
a cord I barely feel ...
                if I release it, if I open my hand,
if I lean deeply in to kiss you, we'll secure
each other, have no need ever
to return,
but something holds, someone whispers, some touch like a
torch falls into the well of me and I

wake to find you gone. Bereft. Void of your touch,
your voice-caress that made confession. (It was,
you said, your deepest secret. I'm blank, cannot grasp it). I
lie on a gurney instead of your bed of
depthless blue, and the silver rails cribbing me, left,
right, might be new-made ice. And only later am I
quit of you, released to try the labyrinth to
where my clothes wait.
Large official clocks stare down to state I was but
briefly gone. Somewhere

the chilled air bares a tooth and somewhere flexes
talons, but you are nowhere to be found
as I flee in throwaway slippers, the thin and shameful gown.

A Walk After Illness

From willows' high window,
uphill meadows pour through.
Blackbird hovers low, its chucking scold an old

motif. *What if*—begins the dread, but red eft
sets a foot on asphalt. *Let me
convey you.* Offer you do not speak aloud.

Writhing from your clasp, the tiny
dragon steps away. To be brief
goddess, intervening, makes the morning mythic,

as does sun from cloudbank, pulled
into sudden clear. O extrication!
Listen, Legs, this walk must breed heirs.

No need to kneel: you've sworn against
squandered days. Two brothers faithful to their fields
farm on Tupper Hill. Therefore the milk truck,

blessing of wave given and received.
(See you again, Driver). Greeting the killdeer
echoes, plaintive in the pasture.

Morning good, Good Morning, your shoes on road
repeat. And the mind's voice counts chimingly:
bay, chestnut, grey. Lovely, their lifted heads. Look,
they drift your way, melodic.

Fragment

May I present my grandmother, the
human burr. Wind's *a cappella* in her ears, the
tears from her eyes twin comet tails.
    A ditch gapes. This—she thinks—
will be her last moment. Notes,
despite her terror, the teasels growing there.
    It's a grave for running water only,
hers still cigarettes away. Not for years,
not till I'm born, and live to hear the tale of
Maude. Not till she's shown, then
saved for me, a set of Limoges plates. (The mare
beneath her clears the ditch,
clatters over a bridge).

Each plate depicts a different flower,
their edges scallop, lively with gold.
Bone china. Her face might be
made of it, too. Fired at the moment the giddy
mare went awry. Many are Maude's moods,
and wear the ribbons of whim.
    Ruth: my grandmother's name.
Maude: the mare's—she's dapple grey or
liver chestnut, she's fifteen hands or seventeen two.
Scar, no scar below one hock,
rough-gaited or water-smooth. Set to
fences, she comes under, or stands boldly back.

Fences. They're running parallel with one.
One/one/one/one/one each post a
white-hot second. Amidst this blaze,
Maude veers; Ruth sees a man, red-sweatered, distant.
    He waves. Did he wave? Idiot, already gone.

They're headed home; were Maude's route
pedigree, it might read as follows:
Short Cut out of Steeplechase by way of No Control.
Ruth ducks low-hanging branches: they're
flat-out through an orchard, grazed
limbs lobbing apples in their wake.

The Limoges? Intact. I'm setting places for dessert.
Plates for eight thudding softly down on mats.
The painter knew her stuff: here's asters
stiffly maned, sweet peas in dishabillé,
an orchid's brazen invitation. And blood will tell, they say,
    I've grown as stubborn as the woman
clinging to the creature
destined to best her iron will. Ask her son who sired me
if this is not so: he's had to endure between us,
like an anvil between blows.

If for a moment you try to envision
survival as aura around the body, you'll
see Ruth low on the neck of the mare, and brilliant,
brilliant just now.

Late November, Last Leaves

Against the pane of pitch black, a pair of
golden hands flattened—a plea or warning.

They fled on wrists of flexing vine she knew
would bring them back. She sat, her
meal over. The scorched shade nearly garnet.

Wind again. There they were.
Hurry, they gestured.

What possessed the dark? She heard her
arguments there, inside
silence so acute she sensed a dress
slip from its hanger. She lit a cigarette. Felt she could
divine the fall of dust.
Confetti from the party
Time was throwing at her expense.

Deeper drags. Her eyes opened. Not yet midnight
though the window was. Her despair
squared with looking.

If, signaled the golden hands,
(torn away, returning)
if you would love again,
love now.

Radioactive Iodine Uptake Test

We met in the waiting room, gripping magazines.
Reading without comprehension page after page.

Blue walls can freeze. Their coldness summoned fiends
whispering banned words. That word "stage,"

once loved, once linked with theater, strutted
murderous. I must have sighed; my glance caught

yours. With quick forefinger you mimed a cut
made at the base of your throat. Overwrought,

you strove for self-mastery by way of a joke:
"I see we share the same necklace." We traded smiles—

wan ones, but they thawed us. Low-voiced, we spoke
as we sat. Was our wait brief or a long while?

Smiles again. Pause. Who was your surgeon?
Same as mine! Fine doctor, we agreed. The best—

you'd researched them all. I saw a secret burgeon
as you said this: nameless thing of conquest

that shadowed, somehow, your candid eyes.
And you named it, let it out of your mouth,

wicked, revelatory as the radioactive dye
that might divulge failure in the room of doubt

we'd enter when called. I would be next,
meanwhile a gasp escaped me, the smallest "oh."

Some might have feared your telling would hex
them for their test, but I thought you might know

an ally when you saw one. There was some look about
me and you took a chance, needing to confess

what you must bear. What possibly you'd fail to rout
you could at least find solace in sharing. What a mess

the whole thing was. Mine hadn't done what yours had;
I might escape. You wanted to break free of your prison.

Saying it aloud, you'd face it squarely, break from bad
enchantment when you found someone to listen.

Where are you now? I wonder. How do you fare?
I've kept you, tended you as best I can. The odd hour

brings you back; your face and voice are in my care.
They're fading—but not the burn, the power

of how you took my fervent wish for luck. I leaned and
took your hand as if I'd known you years, I willed

recovery with my every cell. Cells beforehand
had betrayed us, but what if I could work reversal

just with touch? Absorb, and then ablate your danger?
What if, patient to patient, *we* conceived it, a violent

healing, shocking as shaken faith? I recall voltage
exchanged. Who is more potent than a stranger?

Diana In December

The cloud she wore would soon tear.
She sent a rain of arrows earthward
that turned, as they fell, to flakes. Their
sterling flight swept cedars, dusted horns of the

owl, prompting: Who are you hunting, who?
Colder yet. She never flinched. Merely
nocked another and let fly. In the supple wombs
of does close-gathered, one collective shudder

possessed them, sparked, and died. Their unborn stirred,
the does listened. They could hear granite hunker
as the temperature dropped. Light wind, shirred
by stands deciduous and evergreen, said something.

The people had hung a bell, and it agonized: bronze
mouth aching to close. Mutely it promised to take
back all it had rung. Lit windows cast lozenges
of broken amber, gilding frozen ground. The goddess,

naked now, ran on.

Hotel Sleepless

Pitiless ruby, the smoke alarm's eye. Hadn't
known it would outstare you, sunk in the ceiling's

indifference. Nor guessed microwave light would
wash the room with tyrant lime, phosphorescence

tracing outlines. Cheap clock snacks on
seconds, each bite a brittle *if.* Who was it wove

endlessness into the coverlet stripes? Those ants
that paraded kitchenette tiles are a licorice

stash in walls drunk men pound upon return
with hoots and horseplay. By 4:00 a.m. their

snores chorus, but you press on. Of tears there are
legion: regiments glide from your eyes.

Sheet clenched in hand—look, such perfected nullity:
blank TV, quenched mirror of tabletop, offering a

plate of grapes that cannot tempt. Surrender that
eludes you strokes chairs asleep in their curves,

drapes whose folds absorb quickened breaths of the
dreamer beside you. He is seaside, his spot windless,

afire with the choice of another—sumptuous the
hollow among dunes where he draws her down.

The Gigantic Of Miniatures

Perhaps only the tiniest stars
scattered in grass—
those white ones attached to the frailest of stems—
can show us our true station. And these
hats worn by the mosses, modestly cupped,
touched with rust red,
teach us respect for what we tread,
bend us from a selfish stare
to the lake of deepest looking.

And when our fingers wander among
these blue and purple doors of entry,
five- or four-petaled
(one must count with extra care),
we contemplate some tenderness
quite forgotten until this moment.

There on our knees the deed
comes back to us,
a loving word, a kiss, that burns
the ground and dizzies us,
ringing our lives like a huge, hunchbacked rung bell
up in the massive cathedral's emotions.

Handfuls Of Leaves

Here I am again, wading
knee-deep in family
and friends,
recognizing someone
everywhere.
Tattered, my aunt. Brilliant,
my fifth grade teacher.
No surprise at the shape
my old neighbor
has taken.

Who can hold
handfuls of leaves
without being
burned to recall?
Do I have a face
or is it
a bonfire of letters?

This deep walking as
through waves
parts such a place in me,
I may refuse no one.
Many come to my eyes
helplessly widened
with color,
sing in my ears intent on the
music
a song of ecstasy shaken.

This year
my mother wears scarlet,
my man
a suit of yellow
and whoever comes drifting down
will find me,
waiting and walking below.

White Doe

The Celts believed white deer to be messengers from the OtherWorld.

This is the closest you'll ever come
to a unicorn. (Breathe, don't
breath behind your
window of hemlocks).

Luminous doe in failing light,
among dark others. Listening.
About to turn,
find you out, and speak.

Don't think, she'll hear you. Don't
move a perceptible inch.
Conspiracies of twigs lie
cocked to sound pistol shots.

Why does she summon up old loves
stunning as these first flakes,
settling one by clear-cut one
upon your jacket sleeves?

They whirl and run—she's torn from
you—a page from your journal, but
which one, what day of your
life whose moments ignite

this one? Sunset forces the
clouds apart with sudden
phoenix-light; contrasted flakes
read like ash, blown from huge fires.

If A Blackbird

If a blackbird—wing's flare-red and
cream-crescent out of sight,
his streaky mate tucked
in long grasses—

if a blackbird, his *oak-a-lee*
contained in his whistle-box,
bends stem after stem to bring down
moons of phantom, waning dandelions

if a blackbird—help me, please,
I am repetition and so is he—
if a blackbird ducks his pure night head
in early morning sun
down to a foot, also dark,
to eat the spread of starry seeds,

to feast on the bounty of this day,
may we take it as a sign
to make him magician of every appearance
miraculous and simple?

He conjures this arch of blue held
by keystone of birdsong,
the separate, shining welcome
from each leaf, each blade of grass.

Through him we inhale lilac,
exhale hayfield, as he pulls
handkerchief memories
bright-lined through our minds.

From his epaulet, tiny strawberries
fall to our tranced fingers,
that in the grotto of our mouths we may
taste what is wildest.

And to us he transfers his heat:
sweet coal of summer sun, that our
touch might ignite each other to flames
upon the cool bed.
For he commands our amazing hands,
and all they may do this day.

And if a blackbird, at day's end,
returns to the round of the
new nest, open as a mouth
at the wonders of the world—
if a blackbird, who knows nothing
of what we are forced to know,

swallows only the precious moments
starry and single-purposed as seeds and
converts them by way of his song
to paradise as he knows it

what should we do but follow him?

When he folds his wings upon the flight
Da Vinci once dreamed, he sways on a reed,
tuning up in the hush. A breeze
unfolds; he dips and rows with a few notes
liquidly towards twilight.

Let us have whatever of him
we can possibly manage, let us strive
to loosen our complexities, come
to a place still and serene—
keeping as best we can
within the little clearing of now.

Dead Ringer

Stricken to see her. Wrung by the belle of the
ball fast-forwarded to disco. Rooms gone
mad where spun mirrors made constellations
slither by. Her body writhed and
flashed. The place packed, a galactic seizure.
Distant, she mouthed a message and
you, deafened, missed it, straining through
syncopated space, desperate for her hand.
She loomed to whisper in your ear, and
took you home to melt. The years since then
uncharted, what storm has swept her here?

She summons up the old crowd, unseen they
press you nonetheless, reenacting rivalries
and mouthing extinct favors. Hands in pockets as
they crumple betting lists and phone
numbers, maybe a ticket for parking or a show.
They own your air—you swallow:
the moment Scotch, taken neat.

Not her. You see that now. But Christ, what a
knockoff. Her shape shoplifted, ditto her motion.
That face stamped from the same mint. She was a
lefty; her double holds the coin you need but won't
receive. And even if she tendered to you the
currency of the past, to help you find that
other woman and pay once again,

she'd dance so fast with you she'd spend you,
and she never could be bought.

Magicians, Kindly Honor

Magicians, kindly honor us this evening as we lie
twined in knotted sheets
after the disappearing act.

For truly we were each other
in a coarsely exquisite illusion;
smoothly the flame-dipped movements

incinerated, fell away;
the orange tree bloomed for inward eyes.
Radiant doves spiraled up

                                   wildly,

over our ancestors' heads
from the blue realm where they watched
(deepest corner of our bedroom).

Now, of course, we lie sawn in half
by ragged breaths. We wear the
invisible hats we drew each other out of.

With certitude we contemplate
the returned rabbit of calm
while it sits, pure and intense,

on the ebony table of desire.

Spirit Letter To Rockwell Kent

Dear Rockwell,

The laden spruce you made
sleeps—no, dreams, under glazing
afire with last light. Patience stored in the
pliant boughs in a season linear and sere.
Linear too, your stripes that sweep my
gaze from side to side and launch it into mid-space:
  shadow/snow/shadow/snow.

Snow. Your loaded brush massed up final
whites. Closing on the holiday, you took up
slender sable. Mixed white with cadmium yellow and
daubed till bulbs were strung. By their glow, dusk deepens.

Miles beckon from three lights; I might walk until I
froze. Or reach that welcome and be warmed.
They seduce, but even better is white glimpsed low
and through a gap. How did you know it would
convey me into your tree? I'm looking up,
transported by the limbs' rough spiral. I'm

sucking winter's minted air, straining for
bells. There—hear them? Dark horse that pulls the
distant sleigh, take me.

Yours truly,

III

Spring Snow

Fiddler

(in memory of Johnny Cunningham)

He lifted his fiddle, was away—
we felt the leap in our marrow.
He played us the length and breadth of his
kingdom, face droll then sly. He led us to
laughter, or haunted us into sorrows. He was
burnished by long use, by loves intuited
note for note. He was attuned to the
meander of where he might go.

And though we were his by the easeful hand
wielding the bow, stuck to his violin's honey and
gathered as one sheaf of wheat, though he was
lordly, he suffered, vulnerable as a peeled twig.
Didn't he look us through? Slip away and
come back? Fox who revised his own footprints,
coin come home to known pocket.

Whenever his bow crossed strings, we stacked
stone or knelt in rushes. We heard swans
circle, and saw sleet kiss the sea. We came by
curragh to the shingle—ours was a neat cottage.
We were the hare who leapt from cards held by
Red Hanrahan: distraction to begin, but soon
enough, temptation. Then we were graveyard tree,
branches entwined with another's. Undressed by
rough wind, our roots clasping the buried lovers.

Orchard

Split halves in the lush grass where
yellow jackets tippled, drunk on juice.

If only he would kiss you. But wary
seemed the watchword.

Those trees were wicked, as apples trees
are wont to be. They dropped fruit to

distract him, wove his blue gaze
through their branches.

Gypsies made this furniture, he said.
Made it to sell, and moved on.

Two rustic chairs and a love seat, and
neither of you would sit.

Take me with you! (Tried to say it. Tried)
He looked as though he'd almost heard.

One beat from falling on your prideful knees.
I beg you, love, break stride.

Wind harped the song through your aching head:
Blonde One, let me ride with you, ride.

The Birth Of Keats

Commotion. Berserk shadows when wind
shoved rudely in, forcing the heavy door.
They wild-waltzed with skittish lights
and leaves across the stable's earthen floor

as someone led in a grey flecked with foam,
head a touch Arab, white almond on one hock.
A hostler ran to take the mare. Straw-bits joined the
leaves' dervish seething. His mother felt the shock

of him. Should she fail to endure this pain
dammed at her thighs, she'd die a blocked loop
livid with effort, screams. Knotted sheets for reins,
she'd ride her sweat straight out the Swan & Hoop

doors windows walls roof nothing would hold—why
should she? and felt her mouth stretch formless howl
blood she was bursting midwife said *push*—she gave
who was waiting. Silence. Then his first vowel

climbed, discordant. The hostler rubbing her down
found himself pinned between mare and wall,
crush thieving each breath. Her mass pressed
out lantern light, blotting him, but when all

went sliding-sick a moment, she shifted; he fell
against her, grateful. He breathed anew hay-scent,
saw warmth make flakes mirage in melt: her star-
shaped dapples. She turned, her eye held no intent

of malice; the flare of quick alarm he'd glimpsed before
she sidestepped—exerting to the full her power—
was gone. Whatever she had seen, he honored,
brushing her to satin finish. Late now. The hour

struck three. The mother lay exhausted, firstborn son at
her breast. He stroked on, crooning little gallantries.
Her hair on the pillow streamed black ray on ray. He
combed the pale mare's mane: *There, pretty lass. There, pretty.*

Marion's Mare

In an indoor ring, her mare explores the ways
she can run a circle with bursting bounds.
Three air-borne hooves—the fourth in pocked
ground. Velocity building from phase to phase,

she astonishes air by tipping as a teapot does,
head dropped, heels lifted high—the line from
hock to hoof horizontal. And the insolent tail-
plume curved into a handle. Perhaps because

her joy, immense and smooth, limns all her tonnage,
she appears to float. The only hoof to touch must
soon rise. The door stands open; sunlight makes her
trust the atmosphere in which she levitates. Runs

riderless in light and shadow. The door stands open,
yet she turns and turns within at harrowing speed.
Cloud horse and waterfall horse, whose purpose
needs no explanation of her powers, only the slopes

of fields she conjures, and the pressures of our pent breath.

The Laurel Grove

When I reached the laurel grove, I
found it glimmering
with a weave of titmice and warblers.

The day clasped warmth and cold
together, and the simmer
of possibility brewed in the birds and

they sang. Broken-off notes and
whole notes strung
on thread that tautly crossed and re-crossed

and that passed through me. I
nearly cried, stung
by their sweetness. You recognize your

childhood when you hear it. You are
sounded like a bell:
your innocence before the changes

rung silver, rung multi-tonal.

Greenpoint Woman On Zebra

Wild. Wilder. Wildest. If only he'd
murmur as he used to, resurrect his touch.
She recalls boisterous beds, crush of couch
too small. Showers shared when love's hour
blew horizontal her mind's trees.

Torrid against tiles. Then? Towels. Calm. Sour-
sweet those cigs they smoked, hands damp.
She lies back, kicks out to hear her slippers'
satiny fall. On the night table, bodice rippers,

and on each lurid cover, a woman's escape
or surrender, voluptuous. Downed by cramps,
she's here alone, and where is he? Between the pages,
those women all end up caught. The moonlit phase,
she'd call it. She kills the TV. What's it like to be great?

She gets up, clothed only in perfume.
Ponders, rubbing her belly. To be great,
you must dance, the soul-voice prompts. Elated,
she stamps, throbs. Tidal, she sways, dips, soon her
hair tickles floor; her tight spins swell the room.

Dizzy. But still she gyrates on the faux
zebra carpet. Struts the plush until a doubt
steals her heat. So let him go if he wants out.
She hates what they've become. Where her heart's

drums have gone she would give anything to know.

From "The Dream Manual"

Nepalese painting, 18th century

He dreamt you blue with black stripes,
paws placed on three striped mounds
to show earth's make-up, or to
prove your power colored the
ground beneath you

nothing but red surrounds, the same
red in your ears and mouth,
because listening cups a roar,
because feasting houses a hunger

nothing but red surrounds, the same
red as birth, same as tear-throat death
because life opens and opens
at last

the door of the holy gasp,
where the eye mirrors your appearance in the
chamber of the last breath

he painted you blue with black stripes
in nothing but red surrounds, the red
an eye discerns from farthest distance, where he

painted you, Miracle of Markings,
fire he never intended to fade.

Boa (Close-up Gallery, Central Park Zoo)

They hurry by, but I am lured to stay
by your (non)presence sculpted on faux rock,

your niched world circumscribed by glass,
with rich leaf-litter floor and gridded top

through which a bulb shines to provide your day
of dappled light and tropic warmth. (Night's clasped

unseen in seamless loops). Tied bamboo
strikes a bolt from top to bottom, whose zig

you may ascend as if towards sky. Or zag down
planted tiers of mini-jungle, a rigged

and shrunken version of your realm. You
devour daily mice, drink water found

in the shallows of a glazed ceramic dish.
Sideshow. A hostage of human will

though Medusa might've dropped you
from ringlet-seethe, and bid you be so still

that when I came upon you, I'd wish
to be impervious to your look. To stop

your stone-hypnosis, I'll match you stare
for stare, searching for hesitation, twitch, breath …

Show me none, I beg you. Hold me here.
I crave inviolate peace though artifice.

Hug me as if I were the last of my race: rare,
struggling, savored with terrible fears—

No, don't! Don't tighten your inexorable grip.

Working For Tiger
(Wheat Paste Graffiti, Bedford Ave. at N. 6th St.)

Applied to plywood walls that confine
the construction site, the repetitive cool guy
waits. Arms folded, legs posed to define
hey/pay attention. T-shirt blinding. Jeans pressed.

A fashion assault: continuous line of fifty
or sixty of his image. We falter before him,
fail to discern his features, shape-shifted
since yesterday: over his face someone

has pasted Tiger's, staring with furnace eyes,
his roar Hell's exhalation. You were too slow,
too numerous, Poster Man. Can't parrot words of
lucky ones, reprieved, whose comments flow

by rote when describing how the tiger attacked:
It came from nowhere. Which we might say about
you, Poster Man. Spent, our age of thrift, far back
our careful necessaries, before you led us on to buy

the stuff that chokes the planet. Who thought paper
pulp would render Tiger nearly homeless?
That coffee cups could thirst and food containers gape
to swallow miles of rainforest? But someone

wars on behalf of Tiger, someone offers daily praise
to this god-in-guise our daily hungers threaten.
Over each man-face the features of Tiger, where set
upon set of serial eyes forge a single question.

We flinch in passing. Who can purely meet their gaze?

At Bedford And Grand

Before the old neighborhood's erased,
before it changes utterly,
certain men must move or die, these
pigeon flyers, addicts who've never
kicked the habit of sky
but chase their need up every day
in a ritual old as the Talmud.
   Spirals of pigeons rise,
beget their marvelous sound:
fleet woman in love, ascending stairs
in full-length taffeta gown. Late sun
burnishes the highest birds
to stones flashed in the hand of a jeweler:

diamond   obsidian

        diamond   obsidian.

Meanwhile, a rag-topped pole below
churns in feverish circles,
encoding the air with its set trio of
daily instructions:
Get up there.   Fly around.
Later, come down.
There is a thing called kit pull,
instinct of pigeons to fly together,
tightly, in unison,
pure thought of one mind.
Gaining with its directive power,
magnetism. Drawing stragglers like filings,
subsuming other flocks.

So a flyer loses some birds, wins some,
or the game ends a different way,
as it did this evening, when a pair of merlins
conjured themselves from nowhere. They
strafed the periphery—one seizing a silver dun
whose dying wing beats

so mixed what we, the watchers, saw,
the scrimmage of emotions
crushed everything but awe.

The Complete Works Of Lord Byron

I unpack the book from the box, and at once the poet speaks:

"Gilded and leather-bound, this tome has sat upon his
conscience; he makes his fierce appeal: 'I been clean
seven years!' Gaze on the trackless arms he
extends, elicit from him confession:

Once, he tells you, after a theft, he found his place
in flames, the building roaring. Through din and tumult
he called out to his dog within. And she made answer.
Barred from entry, he fought firemen, then begged.
His dog a torch and a shriek—and he burnt, he said,
with her. Afterward kicked his habit.

Do you recall his tentative knock? See yourself
pouring afternoon tea? You request of him his name, withheld
on other visits. He tells you: 'Pete. But I spell it P E E T.'
Peet. (A fledgling's sound). Only a short time, he says, since
he has learned to read. Children's books. Parts of the paper.
You draw this from him just as earlier I coaxed him to the alphabet,
and to the slow, phonetic handholds he ascends by thus far.
Ask nothing further; accept his gift. Let him
show you his favorite illustration.

But to the present," says Lord Byron, "since we've relived
the past's wonders. Ten years since last you saw Peet. This book
in storage for a decade. Open it. Death has not
changed me; I am still a Romantic.
Read what you will, and find amazement that I'll
wager proves eternal: this pink, pressed rose,
fallen from foxed pages."

Found

While digging holes to plant some tulips,
the long-buried couple turned up:
porcelain doll's leg, unbroken and poignant,
rather than plate shard or handle to cup,

and with it a shooter marble, white,
bearing two concentric rings of red:
an eyeball amazed by the fresh sights,
game-filled, and wise to the ways of the dead.

She wiped off the old warrior and his bride,
whose sock & shoe were marks incised on the leg.
Wiping her forehead, she put the trowel aside,
took off her gloves, stroked the sheen of a twig.

A catbird called. She took up her find, holding
them close in one hand. Knees denting topsoil,
thoughts ablaze in the afternoon's gold.
Catbird improvising. The cardinal, flashing royal.

She bowed her head, listening. Light fell in bands
through mulberry branches, interlaced. Dear
Little Ones, how long you have lain. Hands
are errant wizards. Nothing scours like the single tear.

Lines Written By Someone Else

While I struggled long with an obstinate
line, you'd finished what compelled
in your methodical script.

Dun and dimpled, your back, with
mark of cream encircling black:
a painted eye of forceful stare.

How many of me did you see, how
great was my distortion, ugliest when
from my pen you dodged swiftly
                              and retreated?

Dangerous and impulsive during a
powerless hour, I envied your industry
and all it courted and consented
                to be: intricate, tensile, fabled.

Come out from that crack when it suits,
though my contrition is useless to you,
and my endeavor full of debt I can never make known
                to you nor retract.

Chance me again.

Spring Snow

Wafting upon trees, upon
understory, the history of
lacemaking revises itself. You can

almost hear the song-cycles
of swan migration, feathery
lyrics exploding against the

windshield. And though you're leaving the
territory of adornment and erasure,
though it ceases in the next county

or the one after that, snow
paces itself with your breathing, dips
and rises in you like the road.

The secret? snow says in your ear, *the*
secret is drifting off. The secret? it says again,
fabulous, I forget.

The secret? A breathy voice, androgynous
but lulling. *Would you sully what only*
spirit knows? Traveling onward, you

lose it. But when in May the
spirea shakes down its arcing
snowfall, when from its branches you

pluck a warbler's nest the size of your
heart, touching the lining she made soft,
dappled now with petals, the luck you

were ever born blossoms into voice
O, fallen rice of your parents' wedding, it sings,
O, remembrance till death.

Cloud Company

Head to tail in loose layers, herring
packed with herring. Top hats ringed by genial smoke.
Cherub dwellings, naked women, the derring-do of
little dragons, parted from their dams by
wind's samurai stroke.

They kept happening; the sky lies low and intimate here.
Not like far, faint city skies. Nor like England, said Colin.
But oh, Spain! cried Sally—flicking her napkin,
fending off a moth intent to interfere—
the sky of Spain is truly foreign!

Look! We said, still pointing. Pure Tiepolo,
said Rita. Inevitably, Constable's name came up.
Tony seized on Ryder, Gail mentioned Corot,
meanwhile the clouds ignored us,
busily mating to corrupt

slate blue (shot with orange), and twenty shades
of oyster, dreaming nacreous tints of pearl.
Cerulean holes in smouldry Hades
stared us down, and the sky like drink
dissolved the sun to grenadine swirl.

Tough to get with watercolor, commented Gail,
or with oil, unless with glazes. But egg tempera
was a different story, less likely to fail
when one sought to emulate heavenly light,
to capture translucent phases.

Wine glasses empty, dessert melting, we remained.
Mesmerized by those overblown hourglass sands.
Rush on mercurial rush, achingly sustained.
Massed up sorrows, joys.
The unnerving dispersal of plans.

Umbrella

Zzzzunnck! That slight, concussive note,
tinged with faint inquiry.
A forced bouquet of struts blossoms.
Your mother walks a small town sidewalk
in the first prints of rain.
It was amethyst, that umbrella,
especially under a streetlight;
the fine check printed upon the cloth
had a wonderful name: tattersall.

Umbrellas used to be made with
sixteen struts; now they're made with twelve.
A strong wind, and you're blooming backwards,
clutching a foolish stem. Rain on your head,
throat, hands; the subtle spreading of your shoes.

That umbrella! Gone for so long.
And its closet companion,
stone marten stole that your mother never wore.
Yes, and that closet, that house where strangers
have already lived for years,
your mother herself, whose musical walk
held something racing in restraint,
whose abandoned laugh still sounds
in the labyrinth of your ear.

The past recedes like a buoy,
long observed from the ferry's stern.
Or magnifies, with sensual lens,
the closet dark within: one of those
evenings of hide and seek,

marten fur coolly electric
against your cheek, your hand
stroking the sewn pelts
while the players search—
and wouldn't you know it? Loss
is among them, and finds you first.

Promethea Moth

On her wings she wore eyes of surprise, and was herself
an optic confection, for the hand of the moth god had
sugared her scant but sprinkled cinnamon without stint.
Caught, she beat like a book, pages flipped by wind.
No spider. Instead, she'd snuff by exhaustion.
We imagined her twirl-to-tatters dance

as she fought, tethered by single wing.
The abandoned web held; she spun on
gobbed thread. How then to loose
but not to tear her? Painter's wife, I chose a brush
as from the Nether-Wherever,
Turner and Constable watched my strokes. Marin
pursed his mouth as I worked further under her
wing. When she dropped in the little bucket
cleaned for this maneuver, Kline and de Kooning
grinned. You secured the plastic lid, then handed
me her prison. Attuned, I registered no flutter,
yet each step felt seismic.

The bark good for camouflage, only a cherry tree
would do. Not this tree, I said, not that one,
as we crossed the lane, the downed fence. Did I say she
was big as a child's hand, that our night light drew her? Did I
mention how she began as *it*, strove awhile as *he*,
how somewhere in the struggle *he*
morphed to emerge as *she?* Our theory of her sex
determined solely by the drama.

She clung a minute to the tree we chose.
Closed. Opened, throbbing slow. She flared,
flew us to field's edge, and then she let us go.

Wild Ducks

Dissonant music of come hither recalls three I'd
forgotten: decoy carvers named Heisler, Fitzpatrick,
and English. Men honing shapes to spells to lure down
hen and drake. Look how the flock lowers, as one
body will seek another. Love is part cunning,
part care. Does a decoy carver destroy or
preserve? Yes, says a voice. And Yes.

Have you heard the landing song? In air it skirls
and in water fizzes. Notes of olive or yellow.
Red notes, maybe. Or black. Whatever color, the
skimming feet make bevies of bubbles: eyes
infinite and wise, and I think they imagine me blissful,
buoyant in the womb before I'm put through my
history, before I stand in front of stones to read my
parents' names in granite. Their graves close to those of
Heisler, Fitzpatrick, English. Names of makers.
Names whose linkage brings me wistful music.
And I wonder if you've heard the

fluent dead speaking Brant? Did you get the letter
in Merganser? Or was translation lost?
Today the guns are silent. Across the pond
comes longing. Listen. Your
name is changing shape. At times sunlit
and solitary, at times dark among others.
Watch water brim; see it silver and
shiver and touch both shores.

The Muskrat

While I stood watching, the water began to well,
yielding up circle after circle, and presently
the sorcerer rose sleekly from beneath
and broke the surface. Not the end of the spell

but the outset, beguiled by the way the dark
head plied the blacker surface and the back's
bit of island followed wherever it led. From the
bank above, I spied down. I had embarked

without knowing upon my own erasure. Gone
into ripples ringing outward. Dipped in bliss.
Water like ink held me in a world unwritten.
The buoyant one shimmered and shone.

Notes

"The Blue Tiger Reigns In The East": According to Chinese belief, five tigers, each assigned to specific realms and to dominance within a certain season, exist to "defend the spatial order against the forces of chaos" (A Dictionary Of Symbols, by J. E. Cirlot). The blue tiger's realm is the east, and its dominant season is spring.

"Ming": is loosely based on events that took place in New York City in October of 2003, where a man named Antoine Yates was keeping a tiger and an alligator in his Harlem apartment. Ming was the tiger's actual name.

"Icarus In Reverse": The words uttered by Daedalus are a direct quote from "Bulfinch's Mythology – The Age Of Fable" by Thomas Bulfinch.

"An Evening For Joseph Cornell": Joseph Cornell (December 24th 1903 – December 29th, 1972) is an American artist noted for his collages, boxed assemblages, and films.

"Fiddler": Red Hanrahan is a folkloric character appearing in a number of stories by William Butler Yeats. Yeats drew his inspiration for Red Hanrahan from the life of the bard Owen Roe O'Sullivan (Eoghan Ruadh Ó Súilleabháin).

"Greenpoint Woman On Zebra": Greenpoint is a neighborhood in Brooklyn.

"The Birth Of Keats": The poet John Keats believed that he was born at the Swan and Hoop Inn, where his father worked as a hostler in the stables adjoining that dwelling. Horses have been considered clairvoyant in the cultures of many countries.

ABOUT THE AUTHOR

Margot Farrington's previous poetry collections are "Rising And Falling" (Warthog Press) and "Flares And Fathoms" (Bright Hill Press). Her poems appear in a number of anthologies, and in literary magazines and journals. Other written works include interviews, essays, and reviews. Grounded in professional theater, Farrington is a poet/storyteller/performer whose work encompasses both traditional and experimental modes; she has read and performed widely in venues that include museums, colleges, and literary series, working alone and in collaboration with her husband, the painter and media artist Tony Martin. She divides her time between Brooklyn, NY, and Treadwell, NY.

Free Scholar Press™

Is dedicated to the publication of work both scholarly and imaginative by writers not necessarily affiliated with or otherwise supported by conventional intellectual institutions. We welcome submissions of the highest caliber from independent scholars and creative writers. For more information, visit our website:

www.freescholarpress.com

Also from *FreeScholarPress*™

The Wagner Complex: Genesis and Meaning of The Ring
by Tom Artin, 2012
www.wagnercomplex.com

March On!
by Tom Artin, 2013
Photographs from the March on Washington for Jobs and Freedom,
August 28, 1963, with an introduction by the photographer
www.marchon2013.com

Emil Artin's Iceland Journal, 1925
edited and with an introduction by
Tom Artin, 2013
www.artinsicelandjournal.com

Emphemera & Other Poems
by Tom Artin, 2013
www.freescholarpress.com

26301336R00064

Made in the USA
Charleston, SC
02 February 2014